God's Word for Me

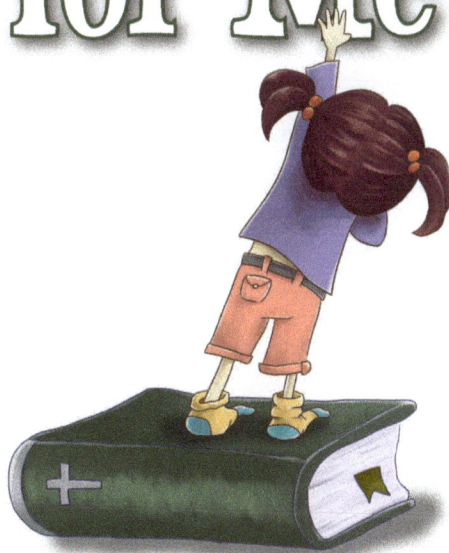

14 Key Verses for Children
on God's Word

**BIBLE CHAPTERS
FOR KIDS**

God is pleased when
I obey His words and
spend time with Him
in prayer.

"Blessed are those who keep
His testimonies, and that seek
Him with their whole heart."

(verse 2)

I read and treasure God's
Word. When I study it,
I can learn about doing
what is right.

"Your Word have
I hid in mine heart, that I
might not sin against You."

(verse 11)

When I read God's Word,
I take time to think about
it, so I can be sure of
what do to.

"I will meditate
in Your precepts,
and respect
Your ways."

(verse 15)

I enjoy reading
God's Word and I
do my best to live it
every day.

"I will delight
myself in Your statutes: I
will not forget Your Word."

(verse 16)

Dear God, help me
to clearly see the
wise and wonderful
things that are in
Your Word.

"Open my eyes,
that I may behold
wondrous things out
of Your law."

(verse 18)

God's word is full
of good advice,
which fills me
with joy and
happiness.

"Your Testimonies
are my delight and
my counselors."

(verse 24)

Dear God, help me to understand what I read in your word, so that I can do my best to follow it.

"Give me understanding, and I will keep your law; I will observe it with my whole heart."

(verse 34)

God's Word helps me to think
more about others, rather
than about my own desires.

"Incline my heart unto
Thy testimonies, and not
to covetousness."

(verse 36)

When I disobey, things don't work out well for me. I have learned from my mistakes and now I follow Your Word.

"Before I was afflicted I went astray: but now have I kept Your Word."

(verse 67)

God is eternal, and so is His Word. I can depend on it forever.

"Forever, oh Lord, Your Word is settled in heaven."

(verse 89)

I love to read God's Word.
I think about it a lot as I
go through my day.

"Oh how
I love
Your law!
It is my
meditation
all the day."

(verse 97)

Honey
filled
Stories

God's Word is a sweet
comfort to me. It can be even more
pleasurable than tasty sweets!

"How sweet are Your words
to my taste. Yea, sweeter than
honey to my mouth."

(verse 103)

God's Word is like a light that shows me the way to go. It shines brightly to guide me in the right direction.

"Your Word is a lamp to my feet, and a light to my path."

(verse 105)

When I spend a lot
of time reading God's
Word, I feel at peace and
nothing can trouble me.

"Great peace have they
which love Your law: and
nothing will offend them."

(verse 165)

Fun Facts

Check out some of the *different* names for God's Word in this chapter of the Bible.

TESTIMONIES

WORD

More books in the series:

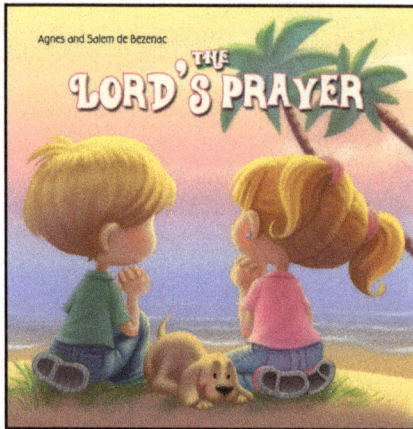

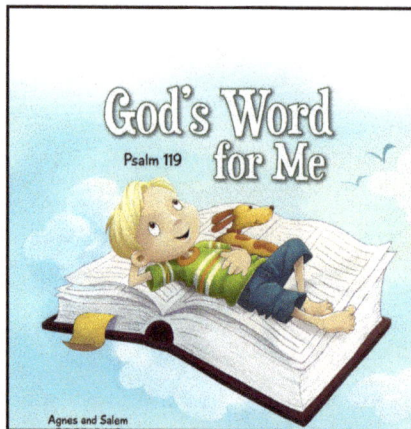

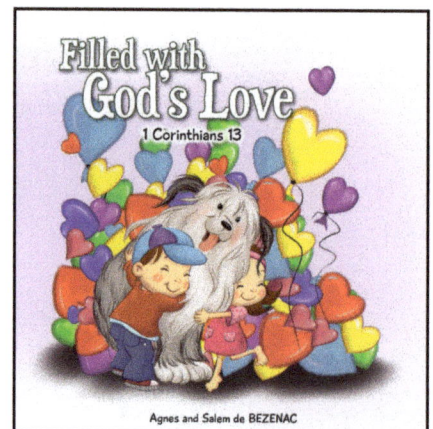

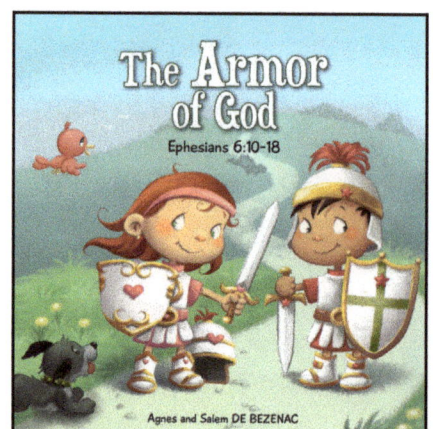

iCHARACTER

Published by iCharacter Ltd. (Ireland)
www.iCharacter.org
By Agnes and Salem de Bezenac
Illustrated by Agnes de Bezenac
Colored by Fiona P and Henny Y.
Copyright. All rights reserved.
All Bible verses adapted from the KJV.

www.ingramcontent.com/pod-product-compliance
Lightning Source LLC
Chambersburg PA
CBHW040250100426
42811CB00011B/1220